Contents

PREFACE TO SECOND EDITION

The points at which the present text is significantly different from that in the fourth impression of the first edition are marked with a marginal line. There are a few other changes, not marked, intended to improve the clarity or style. No claim is made for comprehensiveness, nor are the contents intended for use in any legal connection.

Some activities may require expenditure on equipment or facilities, including proper maintenance, if they are to be conducted with due regard to safety. Whether that expenditure can be made will, of course, depend upon the funds available and the other calls upon those funds. What is clear is that an activity should not be undertaken without adequate safety precautions, and if the necessary resources are not available then the scope or location of the activity should be curtailed so that precautions which can be taken are properly matched to the hazards likely to be encountered.

Responsibility for safety in maintained establishments rests with local education authorities, and in direct grant or independent establishments with governing bodies or proprietors. While every effort has been made to give the best advice available, after consultation with the many authoritative organisations concerned, no claim is made for comprehensiveness, nor are the contents intended for use in any legal connection.

1

Safety on Land (mountain and outdoor pursuits)

General considerations

The number of young people taking part in adventurous activity in mountainous and remote country has risen sharply in recent years. The purpose of these expeditions and the attitudes of those in authority vary enormously. Some parties are from schools, others are composed of young people who have left school; some have the experience of national organisations to support them, others are informal groups. Whatever their composition or purpose, certain basic principles of safety should be observed; it is with them and with the safety practices to which they give rise that this pamphlet is concerned.

The quality of leadership is vital. Experience and sound judgement are the most important constituents; whenever possible they should be reinforced by a nationally recognised training qualification.

There is no short cut to the acquisition of skill and knowledge in the selection and use of equipment and in coping with the natural elements.

The quality of personal and group equipment must be beyond question and should conform to the standards recommended by responsible agencies.

The correct procedure and conduct for any expedition party should be well known by all participants. Progressive and continuous training is a vital feature of any programme.

Safety on expeditions

Expedition work is a normal outcome of camping, climbing, caving and skiing activities in schools, youth clubs and colleges. By far the greatest number of accidents occur on expeditions into mountainous country. This is not only because more people are involved, but because in good conditions the activity appears deceptively simple and safe. The dangers are not always obvious and may not become apparent until some time after a wrong decision has been taken. Without knowledgeable leadership or the right equipment and clothing an unpleasant experience can turn into tragedy. It is disturbing that serious accidents often happen because those responsible disregard the considerable knowledge and expertise so readily available.

1

Equally important for any successful expedition are meticulous organisation and advance planning.

The following points are intended to serve as guidelines. Emphasis will vary according to individual requirements:

Once the *aim* of an expedition is clear, there is no substitute for *first hand knowledge* of the area. At least one person in authority, preferably the leader, should be familiar with the district and the local conditions likely to be encountered in bad weather.

Training programmes should include a thorough course in the techniques and skills of safe movement in open country and in the management of equipment. This will not only inspire individual confidence but will have a marked effect on the corporate spirit of the party.

The principles governing the *choice of equipment* should be determined early. Financial considerations may be important, but terrain, climatic conditions, the degree of mobility necessary, and the available transport should be the major factors in selecting equipment (see list on pages 16-18 and bibliography on pages 14 and 15).

Catering skills and satisfactory diet are important factors in the maintenance of morale and general fitness. Weight, cost, acceptability and simplicity of preparation need to be considered in selecting food-stuffs, and knowledge of dehydrated foods may be valuable. Flexible planning is essential since weather conditions often dictate changes in the menu. The safe handling of stoves in all conditions should be practised, including the technique of cooking in the tent doorway. Parties should always carry emergency packs which, if wrapped correctly and undamaged, will keep for years, though they should be checked before each expedition. Eating small quantities of energy-giving foods during the day is beneficial and, especially in adverse conditions, should not be neglected.

Advice on *insurance cover* is difficult to give since LEA practice varies and standard policies are not always sufficiently comprehensive. It is therefore wise to check such matters as.

Public liability
Personal accident benefits (professional and voluntary staff)
Medical treatment etc
Transport and passenger liability
High risk activities (often excluded from standard policies)
Damage to or loss of personal or hired equipment

Parents should be fully informed of the kind of activities contemplated and, if school pupils or other minors are concerned, their consent to the children's participation should be obtained in writing. Any disclaimer of liability should be accompanied by an assurance that every possible care will be taken. Organisers should be assured of the general physical fitness of all members of the party.

The main hazards in the field are:

Exposure of the body to progressive cooling as a result of severe weather conditions. Cold, wet and windy weather can lead to loss of body heat accompanied by a progressive deterioration of body condition known as hypothermia. It can occur at any time of the year on British hills, even to a strong and fit person. In extreme cases it rapidly results in death unless symptoms are recognised quickly and immediate preventive action is taken. The symptoms are:

A slowing down of pace or effort—though this sometimes alternates with unexpected outbursts of energy.

Aggressive response to advice.

Abnormality of vision, and stumbling.

Slurring of speech.

Shivering and tiredness.

Individually, or in any combination, all these are indications of the onset of hypothermia. If the victim is either urged to greater effort or left unprotected, the consequences can be serious. The most effective action is to stop where the best shelter from the wind can be gained and to insulate the casualty against further heat loss until help can reach him. Additional clothing, even over wet garments, can help. Energy foods and hot drinks could help the victim, and should his breathing stop, mouth-to-mouth resuscitation is vital. If suitable protective clothing is chosen in the first place, if the route is carefully planned to include adequate escape routes, if young people are well trained and if local weather forecasts are seriously studied, then in most conditions the dangers of exposure are reduced to a minimum.

Navigational and map reading errors leading to unforeseen changes of route. These may expose a party to highly dangerous situations, which could end in disaster. An expedition card with a brief outline of the route proposed should always be left at base, or with a responsible person if the base is unmanned. If in emergency an alternative route has been taken, contact with the base should be made as soon as possible.

The following standard procedures should be known to both leaders and members of a party for use when lost:

The leader must keep the group together, remain calm and assess the fitness of the party to move on in the conditions prevailing.

He should find out if possible from the map the approximate location of the party and consider whether to await help or to move on.

If the decision is to move on, an approximate route should be decided on and then held by compass.

If mist prevents the position being fixed, an attempt to descend below the cloud should be made. Every effort should be made to descend open shoulders and the descent should not be hurried. It may be necessary to protect the leader with the emergency rope as the party progresses. When clear visibility is reached, a resection, using identifiable features, should help to decide direction of travel which should then be held by compass.

If darkness is approaching, or a member of the group is exhausted and cannot continue, preparation for a night out must be made. The party should be settled as comfortably as possible using both natural shelter and emergency equipment. Should the weather be very cold, arms and legs should be frequently exercised and care taken that nothing is restricting the circulation of blood. Boot laces should be slackened.

The International Distress Signal (blasts on a whistle, flashes of a torch, or movements to attract attention, in groups of six) should be known and used to guide a possible rescue party.

When the party has reached safety, word should at once be sent to base, to the original destination or to the police.

Retreat from potential danger. A decision to turn back is often difficult to take but wiser than placing a party in a position of risk. In retreating, skill in rope handling on steep ground may be vital to the safety of the party. An emergency rope should therefore be carried at all times. A party should never split up unless there has been an accident.

Ice, snow and wet rock. Accidents occur most frequently on wet rocks and in ice and snow. Movement in mountains in such conditions should be attempted only by parties wearing suitable foot-gear and well practised in the use of rope; for snow and ice prior training in the use of the ice axe and the 'deadman' belay (and possibly crampons) is essential.

Rivers in spate. A few hours of heavy rain can make river crossing dangerous and it should be avoided except in extreme emergency; it is wiser to make even a long detour to use a bridge. If a crossing is unavoidable, a rope should be used. Accepted methods of crossing should be known and practised; details are contained in the publications listed in the bibliography. The possibility of distress from exposure after crossing should not be overlooked.

Fear and apprehension. In unfamiliar situations, especially where there is an element of risk, some people easily take fright. An understanding but prompt and reassuring approach is necessary since even a single affected person can put a party at risk.

Contaminated food or water. Prevention is better than cure. The general health of the party and strict routines for sanitation are of the utmost importance. Water from an unknown source should always be boiled or sterilised by tablets before use for drinking or cooking.

Inconsistent weather. British hills are noted for the inconsistency of their weather. The dangers associated with the rapid developments of fronts and depressions, which often bring arctic conditions, should never be under-estimated. By means of TV, radio, newspapers and local meteorological offices the local weather forecast should be known and if possible ex-perienced local advice sought. Ability to bivouac and to prepare a snowhole may prove vital in an emergency arising from sudden changes in the weather.

Blisters. Good foot care should be encouraged at all times. Frequent examination for blisters should be carried out, and their causes traced if possible.

Loose rocks. When moving on rock or scree slopes and in gullies there is always a danger from loose or falling rocks. Parties should be familiar with group organisation and procedures, especially when negotiating such terrain.

Expedition activities
Mountain walking
Possession of the Mountain Leadership Certificate gives a good indication of a leader's technical competence to conduct parties in mountainous or remote country. Teachers and youth leaders should be encouraged to train for this basic certificate, but whether they possess it or not it is the clear responsibility of local education authorities to satisfy themselves that those in charge of young people have been suitably trained and have the necessary

skill and experience. It is equally important to recognise that the MLC provides evidence only that the holder has attained the minimum standard of competence and experience to organise mountain walking and camping expeditions in summer conditions. It does not qualify its holder as an instructor for rock climbing nor for leading expeditions in winter conditions (which might arise at any time in some mountain areas). It should also be emphasised that the holder of this certificate may not necessarily have clarified his educational aims nor indeed have acquired the qualities of leadership to achieve them safely and efficiently. Nevertheless such qualities need to be confirmed in those who organise challenging activities for young people in any hazardous environment.

Irrespective of the need for a policy on suitable qualifications it is the responsibility of the LEA to ensure that young people receive appropriate educational experience and to establish progressive in-service training for teachers and youth leaders which will provide substantial experience on completion. To achieve this it is important for LEAs to have specialist advice readily available and to provide guidelines on qualifications and procedures required for training and expedition planning. This would establish a 'responsibility chain' to deal with the graded levels of expedition into certain areas and to provide the necessary network of appropriate specialist contact.

The value of progressive training in all outdoor skills for young people in schools and youth organisations cannot be over-emphasised, since the strength of the party will usually be that of its weakest member. A vital element in party safety is the development of initiative in each member, who should always be clear about his own role and responsibilities within the group. To operate effectively within generally accepted safety margins and staffing ratios groups of four or five are ideal, each member being expert in a specific role but able to take over others at need. The size of the group is of the utmost importance, since the minimum may become the maximum in difficult conditions. Four is in general the effective minimum since in case of accident this number permits one member to stay with the injured person whilst the other two go for help.

The inclusion of two members who know the locality and who are selected for their competence to operate in a chosen area will add greatly to the safety and welfare of any group on the hills; if a party has in emergency to split up, it could be vital. The central importance of a progressive scheme of training to develop the skills of safe movement and in living comfortably on the hills, however, should be recognised. From the early stages, if adequately supervised and monitored by suitably qualified and experienced leaders, such training may lead to a level of competence at which young people can progressively plan and carry out their own expeditions. In developing the competence and initiative of individual group members this progressive training, executed if necessary on lower hills or in terrain presenting relatively few hazards, has a vital role to play. Those responsible for the training programme should create frequent opportunities for monitoring the progress of groups, by observation where possible, and by periodic checks and meeting points. It is equally important to ensure that, even when the expedition party is accompanied by the leader, the individual members are given consistent practice in the relevant skills of map reading, navigation and decision making.

Training in mountain walking skills must include accurate judgement of pace, and the mastery of that rhythm and balance necessary to safe movement and to conservation of energy. Except in emergency a party should always work as a single unit; no one should be allowed to straggle behind since this can intensify feelings of exhaustion and depression. Running downhill can be highly dangerous. When descending a scree a group should be so positioned that loose stones dislodged in movement do not prove a hazard to others.

Rapid changes in the weather are a serious threat to the safety of a party in mountainous country. Route cards left at base giving details of compass bearings and estimated times of arrival at intermediate and terminal points are then of special value. Emergency routes should be decided on before leaving and bad weather alternatives should be recorded on the card. If they are adopted for any reason, base should be told as soon as possible.

Good equipment in sound condition is vital to mountain safety. No party should venture on to the hills in weather which is rough or may deteriorate without checking through the basic essentials of personal and group equipment. On expeditions of more than a few hours in rough or remote country everyone in the party should carry a map, compass, torch, whistle, rucksack, large heavy-duty polythene survival bag (500 gauge), first-aid kit, emergency rations, and food. In addition an anorak, spare warm clothing, woollen hat and gloves should always be available. In winter an ice axe and goggles should be carried (see overleaf). The leader should always have a comprehensive first-aid kit, an emergency flare, a 120 ft. length of rope and a duvet jacket or sleeping bag. The effects of wearing waterproof and other garments should be understood so that, especially when labouring uphill, they are used intelligently.

Mountain walking in winter

This demands fitness, stamina and determination. Severe conditions call for more efficient windproof clothing. In snow, navigation is much more difficult, and movement requires greater strength and skill. The danger of becoming benighted is far greater in winter and no leader should expose a group of young people to such a risk. Late starts are often a prime cause of such situations.

The leader's responsibilities are much more demanding and only a skilful and experienced winter mountaineer should attempt to lead young people into the British hills in winter. Even then it is advisable to keep to lower routes where emergency action can be more readily taken.

Each member of a party must know how to carry and use an ice axe safely and should be competent in cutting steps, both up and down, and in traversing; this is achieved only by considerable practice. From the outset young people must be taught the basic method of arresting a fall. It is unwise to allow anyone to walk over snow- or ice-covered streams or rivers, and when moving near ridges and heads of gullies care must be taken to avoid cornices, which could break away several feet from the edge. Experience in the use of a rope is essential in case dangerous areas of snow and ice have to be negotiated. If it seems likely that to go on means prolonged and extensive use of the rope, the party should retrace its steps and move off the mountain.

In addition to being a skilful ice and snow climber the leader must know when it is safe to glissade. For young people this is a dangerous practice and not to be encouraged since a slide can very quickly get out of control and end in disaster. It should never be allowed unless the leader has made sure that there is a clear run out at the bottom of the slope where it is possible to come to rest without harm.

Campcraft

The skills of campcraft are vital to the safety and success of an expedition. Choice of tent and techniques of siting and pitching under all conditions require considerable practice and experience. Tents vary greatly in quality and design and careful selection is necessary to ensure stability and complete protection in the worst conditions. In mountains it is advisable to have an 'A'-shaped tent, with sewn-in ground-sheet and a down-to-earth fly-sheet giving complete protection all round. Good ventilation is essential to reduce condensation and to prevent danger from fumes if cooking has to be done inside a tent doorway. Each tent party should be a self-contained unit. Cooking, equipment and food should be apportioned to cater for the separate needs of each tent group. Team work, skill and experience will affect the conditions of living in a tent. Systematic procedures concerned with sanitation, the organisation of food and equipment and economy of movement under canvas will all contribute towards acceptable standards of safety and hygiene. In camp the most common causes of accidents are boiling liquids, the careless use of tools and the mishandling of heat sources. Cooking in a tent doorway calls for a high level of competence and a minimum of movement, and absence of skill can lead to a lack of hot meals, with a consequent lowering of morale and health.

Stoves and utensils should always be made stable by the use of flat heavy stones. Great care should be taken when exchanging butane cylinders or re-filling pressure stoves. These operations should never be carried out in or near the tent or near a naked flame. No inflammable materials should be stored near the cooking area.

In the choice and preparation of the site it is wise to expect the worst possible weather and every precaution should be taken to ensure that the party stays secure and dry under all conditions. Tents should be pitched to allow free movement between them and to prevent risk of fire spreading. The ability to live safely and comfortably with no more canvas or equipment than can be carried by a team on foot requires a high degree of competence, skill and preparation.

Exploring the locality

Hazards in the immediate environment of a camp are often less predictable than those met *en route* to a site. A leader must indicate clearly to his party under what conditions groups may explore the surrounding area in their leisure time. Unaccompanied parties should not be less than four in number. The leader should be confident that they will act responsibly and remain together when outside the camp boundaries.

Special care should be taken about bathing or swimming; such activities are unwise if the water is very cold or if its vagaries are not known. A teacher qualified in life saving must always be present and it is wise to have members of the group operating in pairs to provide a check on each other.

Rock climbing and safety on steep ground

Rock climbing with young people requires careful grading and must be introduced in easy stages. No one should be fully extended until the basic skills and procedures are fully understood. For beginners a 1:2 instructor/pupil ratio is recommended. Wet or cold conditions naturally increase the degree of difficulty of a climb and this should be fully recognised when dealing with young people. Beginners should be given experience of holding another climber on a rope and of being held themselves. A safety rope must be used at all times in abseiling practice and gloves must be worn when handling 'active' rope. Approved protective helmets must always be worn when rock climbing.

The British Mountaineering Council offers authoritative advice on the selection and care of ropes (see bibliography). Simple precautious to keep ropes in good condition, and points to look for when considering replacement, are clearly set out. It is necessary to keep a careful record of the life and use made of the ropes and to discard immediately any which show signs of undue wear.

The possibility of accidents or emergencies in mountains must never be overlooked and it is essential for party leaders to be familiar with rope management and basic rock climbing skills. They must be able to appreciate the limitations of their party on steep slopes, to assess the potential dangers of difficult terrain and to give competent aid in rescue and emergency. In addition the party leader's ability to deal with rescue operations requiring a safety line can make all the difference between disaster and recovery. Experience of basic rock climbing should include the ability to abseil, to select sound belays and to lead in descent and ascent on easy rock. Training in the use of knots, and practice of the recognised calls and signals required for communication, can be covered indoors.

While there is no substitute for training and experience at the rock face, the recent development of artificial climbing walls offers new opportunities for teaching and practice (see bibliography). Such facilities should be carefully designed. The right materials are essential if anchor points in particular are to withstand the heavy loading and rough usage involved. Regulations and safety precautions should be drawn up locally as these will vary from wall to wall. Regular and careful checking for deterioration at critical points, especially on outdoor climbing walls, is necessary for safety. It is wise to limit beginners to the lower sections. When the use of a top rope is obligatory it must be clearly stated. Access to the wall should be denied unless there is adequate supervision.

Caving

The British Association of Caving Instructors has established a scheme for the training of leaders and instructors. This scheme is recognised as a basic qualification for all who intend to take parties underground. Alternatively, the suitability of a cave leader can be checked with the appropriate Regional Caving Council, if necessary through the National Caving Association. Sources of information are included in the bibliography.

A leader must be an experienced caver. On no account should he take beginners into a cave system which would tax his own ability. In deciding the size of a party he must take into account the degree of difficulty of the system. The maximum safe number recommended is ten, with two adult leaders. If the system demands a reduction in numbers the party must consist of at least four people. The reactions of individual members to unfamiliar situations should be carefully noted by the leader and anyone whose behaviour or attitude might put the party at risk should be excluded. The exploration of a cave is a group activity, but the group should be small, both for mobility underground and to ensure that each person feels himself to be an important part of it.

The basic personal equipment for each caver should include a warm and protective outer garment, stout boots without hook lacing, a protective helmet with chin strap and lamp bracket, and an efficient headlamp. Emergency rations and lighting spares should be carried by the group. Leaders should carry a whistle and a first-aid kit. Wet suits, rope ladders and other equipment will be taken as required to meet the conditions of the trip. Protective clothing and safety equipment must be checked. Details of the passages to be followed should be left at base and leaders should always leave some indication of their presence at the entrance to the cave system being explored. The leader must satisfy himself that there is a wide margin of safety should there be heavy rain while the party is in the cave. The leader and his assistant (who brings up the rear) should have clear lines of communication to keep a check on the condition of the party and to allow a decision to be made to turn back in the event of a mishap. A life-line should always be used when there is danger of a fall.

Surface training should include practice in climbing a ladder in caving gear. All ladders must have life-lines which should be held by experienced and competent cavers. All mines should be treated with the greatest respect and caution; parties should never be taken into coal mines.

Skiing

Where skiing takes place at recognised centres and under resident qualified instructors, graduated training and skilled observation of individual progress is usually assured. The leader of a visiting party should establish adequate liaison with the resident instructors and ensure that their activities are in harmony with his own. He should make sure that the members of his own party are familiar with the local as well as the general precautions and routines.

It is desirable that the party leader should have attended a Ski Party Organiser's Certificate course. These courses are run by the National Ski Federation of Great Britain and cover all aspects of the organisation of school and youth group ski courses.

Groups skiing, both on the Continent and in Scotland, should adopt the following procedures to ensure their safety.

Fitness. Skiing, particularly for the beginner, is one of the most physically demanding sports. It requires a high level of both general and specific strength, endurance and mobility, and a course of fitness training prior to the visit is essential. Party leaders should also ensure that all members get adequate sleep and food during the course so that they are able to maintain the very high energy expenditure required.

Behaviour. Ski parties may visit countries in which alcoholic drinks are more easily available to young people than at home. Special care is needed, particularly with pupils who are under age in this country, if acceptable standards of behaviour, conduct and safety are to be maintained.

Ski equipment. The ski equipment supplied to parties booking through tour operators is normally of an acceptable standard. The length of the skis supplied will depénd on the views of the local ski school. Where possible the skis should be chin height and preferably not more than the skier's own height. Skis should be fitted with adjustable release bindings and retaining straps. The mechanism of the safety bindings frequently becomes jammed by ice and snow, and it is essential to clear working parts regularly.

Ski clothing. To maintain body temperature it is essential that all skiers wear an anorak, ski pants, gloves or mitts, a hat and one or more sweaters. Better insulation results from wearing three or four layers of comparatively thin clothing rather than one or two thicker ones.

To help keep expenditure to a minimum, a pair of heavy duty trousers can be waterproofed using one of several brands of waterproofing material sold in most camping stores. In no circumstances should anyone be permitted to ski wearing jeans.

Exposure to bright sunlight on snow-covered slopes can cause severe sunburn and eyestrain. Skiers should use a screening cream on exposed skin and wear goggles or sun glasses with plastic lenses—not glass lenses which are likely to splinter on impact.

Instruction. Unless the party is accompanied by an instructor of either the National Ski Federation of Great Britain or the British Association of Ski Instructors all groups of secondary age and above should book four hours instruction each day with the local ski school. For those under 11 two hours is more appropriate.

Accidents will be reduced to a minimum if the skiers' code is observed by all. No pupils should be allowed to ski unsupervised, and the advice of local experts should be sought and followed in all matters concerning both on and off-piste skiing.

Many schools now have access to an artificial ski slope. If possible the party leader should organise at least two lessons under the direction of a qualified instructor prior to the visit to the resort. This is particularly beneficial to beginners as it familiarises them with the equipment and the basic skills.

Parties should be adequately and competently supervised and the leader should carry a survival or sleeping bag and a first-aid kit, including an inflatable splint. Care should be taken to ensure that pupils do not ski alone, and expeditions away from the training slopes require that safety precautions basic to safe movement in mountains be observed. Groups operating alone should be aware of the code of conduct set out in the pamphlet *Pre-ski exercise* (see bibliography). It is essential that all programmes are carefully planned and adequately supervised to provide purposeful and profitable activities off the ski slopes.

Riding

Recognition by the British Horse Society will be a guide to the standards to be expected of riding schools when the instruction of school children is being considered. A list of recognised establishments and a pamphlet, *Safety code for riding,* which deals with all aspects of safety with horses, can be obtained from the British Horse Society, National Equestrian Centre, Stoneleigh, Warwickshire. Suitable clothing must be worn, with correct head gear and footwear as basic essentials.

Pony trekking may involve long hours in the saddle and some preliminary riding instruction is advisable. Weather conditions and terrain may make it necessary for protective clothing to be worn. Routes liable to weather hazards, such as unexpected fog or slippery conditions following heavy rain, should not be taken except on reliable local advice.

Visits to national parks

All those concerned with the organisation of visits to the national parks are urged to make the fullest possible use of the service which the national parks youth and schools liaison officers can now provide. They can offer not only detailed knowledge of the area and advice on safety, and on local weather conditions, but also considerable expertise, information and resources which teachers and youth leaders would find extremely useful. Current relevant addresses are listed in Appendix A (page 47).

Use of minibuses

A useful guide for the compilation of LEA regulations has been provided in a leaflet by RoSPA *The use of minibuses by schools.*The following points made in this leaflet, however, deserve some emphasis since they affect the safe use of these vehicles:

1   The entire cost of running the minibus, including payment of the driver or drivers, must be met out of the funds of the owner (or hirer) of the vehicle or one or more of its owners in the case of jointly-owned vehicles. Otherwise the vehicle is subject to public service vehicle regulations.

2   The owner or owners must ensure that there is regular and adequate maintenance of the vehicle to meet the full requirements of the Road Traffic Acts. Records of maintenance must be kept. Except in an emergency, maintenance work should not be carried out within the school or by staff.

3   Drivers of public service vehicles or of any minibus with more than 12 passenger seats must have due regard for the drivers' hours requirements of the Transport Act 1968.

Bibliography

The following books and publications are available from the British Mountaineering Council, Crawford House, Precinct Centre, Manchester University, Booth Street East, Manchester M13 9RZ.

Mountain life (the official handbook of the British Mountaineering Council)

Mountain code (pamphlet on safety)

Hypothermia

Your rope BMC 404

Mountain rescue and cave rescue (the handbook of the Mountain Rescue Committee)

Safety on mountains (CCPR)

Artificial climbing walls (Meldrum and Royle)

Mountain leadership (Eric Langmuir) SCPR

Obtainable from other sources:

Mountaineering—from hill walking to alpine climbing: Alan Blackshaw (Penguin Books).

Expedition guide—Duke of Edinburgh's Award Scheme.

Camping, Education Pamphlet No. 58, Department of Education and Science (HMSO, 170g, 65p).

Be expert with map and compass (Bjorn Kjellstrom).

Handbook for expeditions (The Brathay Exploration Group & Geographical Magazine).

Pre-ski exercises—Ski Club of Great Britain, 118 Eaton Square, London SW1W 9AF.

Manual of caving techniques, Cave Research Group of Great Britain (Routledge and Kegan Paul).

British caving (2nd Edition), Cave Research Group of Great Britain (Routledge and Kegan Paul).

Out and about: A teacher's guide to safety on educational visits— Schools Council (Evans/Methuen Educational).

Public service vehicle leaflet 147. (Department of the Environment.)

The use of minibuses by schools (RoSPA leaflet, address page 36).

Organisation novice caving trips information sheet 1

(The British Association of Caving Instructors—address below).

Addresses

Further information on caving from:

Cave Leadership Training Board (Certification Scheme)
5 St Paul's Street, LEEDS.

National Caving Association (The governing body for caving)
c/o Department of Geography
University of Birmingham, Box 363
BIRMINGHAM 15.

British Association of Caving Instructors
(Cave Leadership Training Board)
5 St Paul's Street, LEEDS LS1 2NQ.

(This association is a constituent part of NCA and is concerned with caving instruction, leadership and education.)

Mountain Leadership Training Board
Crawford House, Precinct Centre
Manchester University, Booth Street East
MANCHESTER M13 9RZ.

Scottish Board:
Mr. Charles Wilde
1 St Colme Street
EDINBURGH EH3 6AA.

Irish Board:
Mr. R. Jones
49 Malone Road
BELFAST BT9 6 RZ.

Safety on Expeditions: Check List

The group

1 Can members of the party use a map and compass with confidence in all the conditions likely to be encountered?

2 Has a route card been prepared giving escape routes, bad weather alternatives and estimated time of arrival?

3 Is at least one member of the party familiar with local conditions?

4 Have local and general weather forecasts been studied?

5 Is the party trained in mountain walking and are the procedures for party movement on free, narrow ridges and steep and broken slopes etc. well known?

6 Is the personal equipment of each member of the party suitable for the terrain and for all the weather conditions likely to be met?

7 Has the camping and group equipment been checked and are members of the party knowledgeable and skilful in its use under difficult conditions?

8 Are the tent groups experienced in campcraft and cooking skills including the use of dehydrated foods? Are they familiar with the planning and preparation of hot meals under difficult weather conditions?

9 Are the members of the group conversant with accident procedures and have they been given routine and essential information in case of emergency?

10 If snow and ice conditions are likely to be experienced are all members equipped with ice axes and are they trained to use them?

The leader

1 Do the leader's knowledge, skill and experience comply with nationally accepted standards of mountain leadership?

2 Does he know the individuals in his party well and can he forecast their reactions under trying and physically demanding conditions?

3 Is he competent in basic climbing skills and river crossing techniques?

4 Is he competent in the treatment of exposure and in first aid?

5 Does he carry the additional equipment recognised as being essential to the safe conduct of the party at all times?

General

1 Are the nature, purpose and aim of the expedition clearly understood by all concerned?

2 Have the parents been informed and are they aware of the activities involved?

3 Does the LEA insurance adequately cover the expedition activities and if not has extended cover been taken out?

4 Has the insurance of voluntary helpers been considered?

5 Has the expedition been cleared with landowners or official departments?

6 Is the party familiar with the country code?

Equipment for Expeditions

Items normally worn for mountain walking

1	Boots	6	Underwear
2	Stockings	7	Anorak
3	Warm trousers (not jeans or thin nylon)	8	Gloves
		9	Woollen headgear
4	Shirts	10	Cagoule
5	Sweaters	11	Gaiters

Items 8, 9, 10 and 11 would be worn as required according to conditions and weather.

Items for summer mountain expeditions

1 PERSONAL
Rucksack
Sleeping bag + inner
Complete change of clothing
Toilet requisites
Mug, plate and cutlery
Knife or
Tin opener
First-aid
Large survival bag—
   heavy duty polythene
Whistle
Map
Compass
Torch (spare battery)
Matches
Plimsolls

2 GROUP (SHARED)
Tent (groundsheet)
Flysheet and poles
Stove
Fuel bottle
Nesting billies
Water bucket
Rations and containers
Washing up (pads, cloths)
Toilet paper
Trowel
Emergency rations

3 LEADER
First-aid kit
120 ft. No. 2 nylon rope
Spare fuel
Emergency rations
Large survival bag—
   heavy duty polythene

Additional items for winter mountain expeditions

1   PERSONAL
    Overtrousers
    Sweaters
    Underclothes } additional
    Trousers
    Scarf
    Goggles
    Ice axe
    Overmitts

2   GROUP
    Mountain tent

3   LEADER
    Duvet jacket
    Emergency flare
    Crampons
    'Deadman' belay

Use of minibuses (see page 14)
At the time of going to press a Private Member's Bill (Passenger Vehicles (Educational and Other Purposes)), which provides for amendment of the law in relation to minibuses, had passed through the Committee Stage in the House of Commons.

2

Safety Afloat

Introduction

More and more schools and colleges make use of the water each year for recreation and study, and as the exploration of its potential for a variety of educational purposes continues this development will expand still further.

Unfortunately, despite the vigorous efforts of the many bodies concerned with water safety, the number of deaths which follow incidents in the UK involving small craft has remained regrettably high. Although few of these incidents concerned schools directly, their persistence points to the need for all who have responsibility for water activities to ensure that the necessary precautions and training for safety are given the highest priority in the organisation of programmes. This is not merely a matter of the self-preservation of those participating; many accidents take place in the presence of bystanders who are unable, for lack of skill or knowledge, to help. Today's schoolchildren will be tomorrow's inadequate bystanders unless effective water safety training is incorporated wherever possible into the routine of their programme of activities afloat.

The main dangers

Training programmes which emphasise the acquisition of skill and confidence on, in and under the water will reduce the likelihood of drowning through panic, but research indicates that even for the strongest swimmer immersion may be attended by a potent danger over which he has little control—the effect of the coldness of the water. Sudden immersion in very cold water may so disrupt the normal breathing pattern as to reduce almost to incompetence a proficiency well tested in a warmer environment. A swimmer whose normal endurance was measured in thousands of metres volunteered to swim as far as he could, clothed for warmth, in water at 4·5°C, but he was in a state of exhaustion within the first 100 metres. The lesson of this and other experiments seems clear: unnecessary exertion when immersed in cold water is to be avoided.

The temperature of open waters in and around the UK is rarely high enough to be sure that immersion will not be accompanied by some degree of shock effect, and there exists a second danger which is also magnified by exertion.

19

Loss of body heat, at a rate greater than that at which the body can itself produce heat, leads to the condition known as hypothermia. Water, displacing the insulating layer of air between body and clothing, may increase the rate of heat loss by a factor of up to 27. This rate is minimised if the clothing is sufficiently waterproof to hold the initial layer of water, warmed by the body, close to it—the principle of the wet-suit—but it is increased again if physical activity causes the water to be constantly replaced. At any water temperature below about 22°C physical exercise in normal clothing is likely to increase the net heat losses from the body. Since average summer sea temperatures around the UK are below this figure lengthy immersion is always to be avoided.

The insulating layer of air may also be removed by strong winds or by wetting of clothes without immersion taking place. The early signs of hypothermia, or 'exposure' as it was commonly referred to, should be known to all who supervise activities in these conditions. Apart from shivering and numbness, the abnormal behaviour which may give warning includes listlessness, lack of co-ordination, weakness, and failure to respond to instructions. Cramp, nausea, and defects of speech and vision have been noted at a later—and very serious—stage.

The possibility of accidents which may involve these two main hazards of water activities—drowning and hypothermia—makes it essential that as many as possible of those taking part, as well as the person supervising, possess the first-aid skills which may be needed and know how to summon professional help with the minimum delay. In the case of drowning, expired air resuscitation and heart massage may be needed, but for hypothermia the basic need is for warmth. Water activities should not be undertaken in extreme conditions unless any victim can rapidly be brought into warm surroundings—preferably a hot bath. After any accident in which the victim has been unconscious in the water, however briefly, first aid should be followed by a hospital visit since the inhalation of the smallest quantity of water can lead to infection of the lungs.

The main aim of safety precautions, however, is to prevent any such accidents occurring by directing the vigilance, skill and knowledge of all concerned towards confining risks to areas in which the learner will profit by his error. The consequences of error in a situation of risk must be clearly foreseen by those responsible, and the facilities and organization must be provided which will ensure that such a situation cannot develop from a valid learning experience into an accident.

The remainder of this chapter offers some guidance on safety precautions drawn up with the help of many bodies having expert knowledge of water activities. No set of rules is likely to cover every possible circumstance, so that the exercise of common sense and knowledge of local circumstances are necessary for their interpretation. A list of bodies from which more detailed information and advice may be sought is given at the end of the chapter.

General

Building boats and canoes and then sailing them are becoming increasingly popular activities in schools, either during school hours or as out-of-school activities. Whatever facilities are available, whatever the purpose of building the craft, and whatever the uses to which the finished craft is to be put, a sound design is the first essential. Many professional designs are available from which craft suitable for instruction have already been built and fully tested. Deviation from a tested design may lead to tragic consequences. A well-built, well-found craft should have a long and useful life and, since depreciation in value is small, the initial cost should not be cut by the acceptance of inferior or unsuitable materials.

The type of water on which a boat is to sail affects the design; ample freeboard is desirable in open water where waves are likely, but too much freeboard increases wind resistance considerably. Lightweight decking may be favoured, but decking adds weight, and if the boat is to be manhandled regularly weight is an important consideration. Whether the boat is to lie at mooring or to be housed in a boatshed, a light, strong hull is desirable. Boats should be carefully maintained and a log-book recording the condition of boats at regular intervals, and repairs done, should be kept. Similar considerations apply to canoes.

Having built or bought a satisfactory craft, the school will want to use her on whatever stretch of water is available, and it is at this stage that the question of suitable precautions inevitably arises.

Supervision

It is essential that activities of this kind should be properly organised and to this end a responsible and thoroughly experienced person (referred to below as the 'director') should be in charge of the party and their activities: he may be a teacher or some other qualified person. The responsibilities of a director might include:

> The conduct and safety of all concerned; for example, checking the condition and suitability of craft and other equipment and deciding whether crews have sufficient experience to go out in the prevailing weather conditions.
>
> Administrative arrangements; for example, insurance, where necessary, of persons and property.

Arranging for instruction and for adequate competent assistance.

The director and his assistants should be fully conversant with local conditions; for example, tide, weather and dangerous features such as weirs. He should guard against dangers arising in connection with large craft operating in the stretch of water his craft will be in. As the area of water available, or the number of craft in use, increases, so will the need for systematic organisation of activities. Routines developed for the control of craft at instructional centres contribute to the safety and the learning of pupils, and offset to some extent the inherent difficulties of communication. The limits within which craft are to work, and a plan of courses designed to achieve practice in specific manoeuvres, should be part of the briefing to all crews. In this way existing conditions of wind and tide can best be matched to the safety and learning requirements, and the areas in which capsizes are most likely to occur can to some extent be forecast. Information on prescribed areas, and courses set, together with the names of the pupils in each boat and their expected time of return, should be readily available to all assistants; a blackboard which also shows weather and tidal information, and recall signals, is useful for this purpose. It should be a duty of each pupil to note this information, and to report his safe return.

Swimming

A degree of competence and confidence *in* the water is essential for pupils who want to sail or canoe. The director should satisfy himself that everyone taking part can swim, in light clothing, a distance of at least 50 metres *in the conditions likely to be encountered.* This is a minimum requirement, and attention is again drawn to the effects of cold water. The distance should be increased to 100 metres if the evidence is provided by a test in an indoor swimming pool. If the director supervises the test himself it is vital that adequate safety precautions are taken; each pupil must be tested separately, either within his depth or closely attended by a qualified life-saver. For canoeing, a basic requirement is confidence *under* the water; the ability to swim under water and to retrieve objects from the bottom would provide some evidence of this, as would the ability to swim through underwater hoops.

Authorities and schools wishing to set a recognised standard of achievement in personal survival could encourage their pupils to try for the Bronze Award of the Amateur Swimming Association.

The director should also try to ensure that everyone can give artificial respiration by the method of expired air resuscitation. Proficiency in this is a requirement for the award of the Bronze Medallion of the Royal Life Saving Society, interest in which should be fostered by any school using the water.

Lifejackets

Everyone, instructors and crew, should wear a lifejacket when afloat.

Lifejackets should conform to British Standards Institute Specification No. 3595/1969, which deals with several different types. The type which depends partly upon built-in buoyancy and partly on oral inflation is recommended as the most suitable for sailing and canoeing. The National School Sailing Association and the British Canoe Union offer advice on the suitability of specific makes of lifejacket. For a lifejacket to be effective it must be correctly worn, and it should be a routine part of the duties of the director or his assistants to check that each pupil has fastened his lifejacket securely and in accordance with the maker's instructions before going afloat. Lifejackets used by schools are subjected to a great deal of wear and tear and those which depend for any part of their buoyancy on inflation should be frequently tested for leaks.

In suitable conditions, such as in a large rowing boat in shallow water, it may seem reasonable or necessary to a director to relax the rule on the wearing of lifejackets. He should do so only as a positive decision for a specific purpose, conscious of the fact that about one person in twenty is *not* buoyant in fresh water, even after taking a deep breath, and keeping the lifejackets ready to hand.

When canoeists are surfing, playing canoe polo, or on a fast-flowing river, they should wear safety helmets and, at the discretion of the director of canoeing, buoyancy waistcoats which give greater protection to the body than do lifejackets.

Sailing

Qualifications of director

It is recommended that the director of sailing should hold a current certificate as sailing master in the national coaching scheme jointly administered by the Royal Yachting Association and the National School Sailing Association. Any assistant whose duties are confined to instructing a single crew should hold the instructor's certificate. In tidal waters the director and his assistant should hold tidal endorsements to their certificates.

Arrangements for rescue

These are particularly important when boats are used in tidal or exposed waters. The director should make arrangements to meet all foreseeable contingencies, and he should make certain that everyone understands them. Local conditions govern such arrangements but they may include:

a. informing the coastguard and harbourmaster (see Coastal Passages, paragraph e, page 29);

b. posting a look-out to keep all boats under observation;

c. having an escort boat under way in a position to effect a quick rescue, or, in fair weather, a power or pulling boat ready to assist without delay.

Escort boat

The first duty of the crew of an escort boat is to ensure the safety of people. However, since one of the important objects of sailing is to foster self-reliance it is necessary for the escort boat to be in the hands of a person of judgement and experience who will encourage pupils to extricate themselves from their own difficulties: he will help to give them confidence by not intervening unnecessarily.

A second duty is the recovery of boats and equipment, and for some schools the escort boat may also be used to accompany expeditions. This potential range of function makes it impossible to specify a single craft which will be the best for all schools. Sturdiness, stability and manoeuvrability are certainly required, with a low enough freeboard to allow easy recovery of people from the water; the speed, power and sheltered space desirable will depend upon the area and nature of the waters in which it has to operate.

Although a powered craft is strongly recommended for this work its propeller constitutes a special hazard, and it may be necessary to use a rowing boat where a stretch of water is shared with anglers or where oil pollution control is strictly enforced.

Detailed guidance and advice on suitable boats and equipment (which should include a supply of blankets in all but the mildest conditions) is available to members from the National School Sailing Association and the School Sailing Association of Wales.

Delegated authority

Whenever a boat is sent out without an instructor aboard it is the responsibility of the director to ensure that one person is in charge and that all aboard are made aware of it.

Recall signals

A simple, unambiguous communication system is essential for issuing general instructions, particularly in the event of unexpected changes in the weather. Distinctive shapes such as cylinders, cones and spheres should be used for this purpose, to ensure visibility from all directions. Their positioning, shape and colour should also take into account the background against which they have to be distinguished.

Clothing

It is invariably colder afloat than conditions ashore suggest. Warm and waterproof clothing should be worn, at least on the trunk, and a dry change of clothes should be available ashore. Anoraks are suitable in most conditions, though their hoods are a hazard if left free at the back of the neck; wet suits are strongly recommended in the winter months and in exposed waters. Light deck shoes or non-slip plimsolls should be worn and *never* on any account should gum boots be worn afloat on small craft.

Capsize

In the event of a capsize the crew should STAY WITH THE BOAT. The routine when a capsize occurs must be thoroughly understood by all taking part in sailing. The procedure should be drilled thoroughly under controlled conditions so that young people know what to expect, and fear of the unknown is eliminated. Crews should be familiar with the hazards and know what to do, e.g. if they are unable to put matters to rights, cut away the mast and rigging in extreme cases, and sit in the boat as though in a bath until rescued.

Boat buoyancy

Boats should be so designed and equipped that they will float and support their crew after a capsize and so that the water can be baled out. It is essential that buoyancy bags or tanks are sufficient and properly secured and that aids such as caulking for the centre-board casing are conveniently stowed. Swamp tests should be carried out periodically to ensure the effectiveness of these measures and to instil confidence in the crews.

Ballast

In heavier craft, moveable ballast should be so secured that it cannot move at all, or should be so arranged that it will fall clear in the event of a capsize.

Equipment

In addition to a full sailing outfit, each boat should carry equipment to meet emergencies, secured by light line. All craft, including light dinghies sailing in sheltered waters, should carry a list of things to do and to check before setting sail. This list should be waterproofed and fitted to the boat or supplied to the cox'n. All craft should also have at least two oars or paddles and the necessary crutches or thole-pins as well as a baler and a knife. Larger craft or those used for estuarial work or more extended passages ought, in addition, to carry the following: a length of light marline or boatlacing; an anchor and warp; a sea anchor when working in exposed waters or where surf may be expected on beaching; a torch; some means of making a distress signal; a boat hook; a lead line; a lifebuoy or buoyant object on a length of line for throwing to a person in the water (this is of particular importance in heavy craft and powered safety boats); and a compass.

The Department of Trade has published detailed recommendations on safety equipment for pleasure craft which should be consulted. They are contained in *The seaway code* which is available free from HM Coastguard, from Marine Survey offices, or from the Department of Trade, Gaywood House, Great Peter Street, LONDON SW1P 3LA.

Canoeing

It is recommended that the director of canoeing should hold the senior instructor's certificate of the British Canoe Union. His assistants should be competent canoeists, and should be encouraged to follow the BCU trainee instructor's scheme.

Preliminary instruction

It is essential that the novice should quickly gain confidence in using a canoe, and this can usually be achieved by first working in shallow water or a swimming pool where his instructor can stand in the water beside him. Capsizing should hold no fear for him, and the necessary drill should be thoroughly mastered before he goes out without an instructor in close attendance. Canoes should keep in minimum groups of three, and there should not be more than eight canoes under the supervision of one instructor (six in open waters).

Stay with the canoe

Unless there is danger from drifting down to some hazard such as a weir or sluice, a canoeist should stay with his canoe in the event of a capsize and either await rescue or swim towards the bank with the canoe in tow.

Buoyancy

Every canoe should be fitted with internal buoyancy firmly secured at bow and stern—27 kg or 60 lb of positive buoyancy in a submerged canoe is recommended. British Standard BSMA 76/1976—*Safety features of canoes* gives detailed recommendations.

Recall signals

Instructors afloat may control their groups by the signals recommended in the manual of the Corps of Canoe Life Guards, but if the director of canoeing is ashore a simple, unambiguous communication system is essential for issuing general instructions, particularly if the weather unexpectedly changes. Distinctive shapes such as cylinders, cones and spheres should be used for this purpose, to ensure visibility from all directions. Their positioning, shape and colour should also take into account the background against which they have to be distinguished.

Rescue arrangements

In all but the most confined and sheltered waters, at least two canoes in a fleet should be manned by people experienced in rescue and rafting techniques. It is important that instructors are skilled in getting a learner back into his own canoe quickly when operating in cold water. In very cold water it is advisable to have a larger boat standing by.

Equipment

In addition to paddles, the following should be carried: a spray cover for the cockpit (this should not be of the type fitted with press buttons; those fitted with elastic bands and release straps are to be preferred: it is important that spray covers should fit snugly over the cockpits); a buoyant painter, fore and aft, with the ends properly secured; a sponge for baling; a repair kit (2-inch industrial PVC tape will be found to effect most temporary repairs).

Expeditions

In recent years small craft have been increasingly used in the mounting of expeditions. These may be little more than a picnic afloat but can include landing and camping overnight. They can range from a week-end spent on a quiet canal to the passage of a river, rapids and all, in canoes, or a coastal voyage from port to port in craft as small as light dinghies. If these adventures away from familiar waters are to be both profitable and safe, some additional precautions are called for.

A considerable body of knowledge and experience in this field has been built up and is available from the following sources:

> The National School Sailing Association
> The British Schools Canoeing Association
> The British Canoe Union

The Royal Yachting Association
(Addresses are given at the end of this chapter).

A greater degree of skill and physical stamina is required for extended expeditions than for an afternoon's racing. It is wise to start passage work in a small way with very short trips and build up as experience and strength grow.

Special instruction

An expedition must be meticulously prepared. In beaching, portaging, shooting rapids and keeping close order, special instructions should be given well in advance and the necessary skills practised. For canoeing on waters rated grade 3 or above the director should hold the advanced certificate of the BCU; for sailing in tidal waters he should hold the appropriate tidal qualification of the RYA or NSSA.

The craft themselves should be brought to a high state of readiness and tested well in advance.

Stowage

The stowage of camping gear and equipment needs care and planning. It is important that craft are not overloaded; care should be taken that trim is maintained and that stability is not disturbed. It will be found useful to stow kit in strong plastic sacks whose mouths can be made airtight by tying securely with light line. If some air is trapped in the parcel, it will not only keep dry but will float if dropped overboard and, if properly secured, it will provide some additional buoyancy to compensate the craft for extra weight. In canoes all gear must be stowed away from the cockpit so that the canoeist is not hampered in getting in and out.

Insurance

All policies should be checked to ensure that they cover the planned activity.

Voyage plan

A plan, with estimated times of arrival and departure, should be prepared, based on the personal experience of the director who should be familiar with the water to be covered. It is wise to prepare a list of 'contacts' with their telephone numbers. These should be, for example, police stations, coastguards, water-bailiffs, lock-keepers, who can if necessary help to maintain communications and, should conditions warrant, keep a look out for the expedition. It is good practice for some one person, not on the expedition, to maintain a 'headquarters' to follow progress. He should always be informed of the times of arrival and departure and of any change of plans. Each craft should possess a copy of the plan and a list of contacts.

When under way, sound seamanship enjoins the rule 'keep together'. Several craft in close company are much safer, since they can support each other, and engender confidence in their crews. The formation of the fleet, and the position taken up by the leader, will depend on the type of water. In rivers the director will normally remain in the rear with the most experienced of the remaining sailors or canoeists leading; apart from these two if the slowest craft are at the head of the formation the group is more readily kept together. In open waters the director of a fleet of sailing craft can more readily control the group from a position to windward, while the director of a fleet of canoes may wish to be to leeward of his fleet so that any capsized craft would drift towards him. While it may not always be easy, there is much to be said for keeping a full and accurate record of events. If this is done on short passages, an abstract of errors and omissions will be of great value in preparing and training for a more ambitious project.

Coastal or extended inland water passages

General
a.   *Life-jackets* should be fitted with a whistle, and conform to BSI specification No. 3595/1969. They should always be worn when afloat.
b.   A *water bottle and iron rations* should be carried however short the proposed time afloat.
c.   *Wind, weather and tide* must be carefully considered. Weather forecasts should be obtained and local advice should be taken. A leeshore or outgoing tide should be treated with great respect.
d.   On coastal passages, *seasickness* must be guarded against and tablets should be carried. Previous experience in rough water but close to refuge should be a prerequisite for anyone joining in a venture of this kind.
e.   *Forms CG66A and CG66B* should be completed and returned to the local coastguard station before a coastal passage is undertaken, and yacht clubs, harbour masters and similar authorities along the route should always be asked to keep watch on a cruising fleet of small craft.
f.   Additional equipment should include *up-to-date charts or maps* and, when off-shore, a *compass* and *distress signals* are essential. Plastic covers will keep these dry. Experience has shown that care must be taken in the choice of pyrotechnics. Preparatory training in use of this equipment is essential.
g.   Most important of all, *crew must be trained in advance* to deal with the hazards they may meet and the director should ensure by personal experience that he knows what these are.

h.   In all but the finest weather on the kindest of coasts, a fleet should always be accompanied by a *powered safety boat* whose duties may well be more extensive than those of a boat standing by a racing circuit. It may be necessary to take crews aboard and to tow disabled craft.

j.   The director should be aware of changes made from time to time in the International Regulations for the Prevention of Collision at Sea. New regulations operate from July 1977.

Sailing passages

It is important that the boats are suitable for the work, that they are rigged with a cruising suit of sails, that sail can be reduced or furled when under way, and that crew are trained accordingly.

Crews should be practised in 'man overboard' drill and in the art of sailing in close order, heaving to and going alongside to transfer personnel, and in beaching through shoal water and surf. All boats should carry oars and crutches, balers, torches, a towing warp and a pyrotechnic distress signal in a water-proof container.

Canoeing passages

Before attempting one of the more difficult inland water voyages or a sea passage, a canoeist should pass the inland waters or sea proficiency test of the British Canoe Union.

Canoes should be of a type designed for work in rough water, whether on rivers or off-shore, and there should be an instructor for every six members of the party.

Canoeists must be trained in advance in rafting techniques, not only to help a capsized comrade, but also to deal with a cramped, exhausted or seasick person who may need to be helped ashore. Beaching techniques are equally important and need prior practice.

It is important to remember the effects of cold water. Even a very fit person can rapidly become chilled when exposed to bad weather and may thus be at risk through loss of strength.

All canoes should carry spare paddles, balers, and a length of light rope and, when on a sea passage, chart or map, compass, and distress flare, all stowed so as not to hamper the canoeist when getting in and out.

Off-shore cruising

For cruises in larger craft capable of longer passages it is less easy to recommend general rules for safety but the following ideas may be of value in outlining the additional hazards to be guarded against and in suggesting the sort of precautions which will prevent mishaps from developing into accidents. These suggestions are as important when considering a vessel for charter as when buying one.

A considerable body of knowledge and experience has been built up and is available from the following sources:

> The National School Sailing Association
> The Royal Yachting Association
> The Association of Sea Training Organisations.

Advice on craft

When considering the use of a vessel for cruising in open water, it is recommended that the advice of the Marine Division of the Department of Trade should be sought on the following points:

a. The suitability of the proposed vessel and what alterations or repairs may be needed to make her seaworthy.

b. The limits of time and area within which she may reasonably be used.

c. The equipment she should carry: the Department's recommendations for craft under 45 feet in length are published in RYA booklet G9/72, but there are statutory requirements for larger vessels, details being obtainable from Marine Division at the address given at the end of this chapter.

d. The number the vessel may safely carry under the various conditions proposed for her use.

e. Any special qualifications which are desirable or required in the person in charge or professional crew which may be made necessary by the size of the vessel or the nature of the voyages to be undertaken.

f. The arrangements to be made for periodical survey and overhaul of hull equipment.

g. A radio receiving set for weather forecasts should always be carried and the Ministry of Posts and Telecommunications should be consulted when making arrangements for radio transmitting equipment.

Fittings

In recent years more accidents to cruising craft have occurred through ill-designed or badly maintained fittings than from almost any other cause. The following are points which it is particularly important to watch:

Cooking arrangements. Unless these are of good design, expertly fitted, surrounded by flame-proof materials and able to hold utensils securely under sea-going conditions, fire, burns and scalds are serious risks. Equipment should be of the type specifically designed and labelled 'for marine use'. Petroleum spirit should never be used nor should any burner system which depends upon atmospheric or wick feed. Stoves which operate from alcohol, fuel oil or paraffin with either pressure or gravity feed are suitable, as are those using butane gas. In the latter case, care must be taken to ensure that all connections are in good order and are tight. Ventilation of the bilges to avoid the accumulation of explosive gas mixtures is imperative. Danger alarms to warn of the presence of gas in the bilges can be obtained quite cheaply. Main fuel cocks should be turned off on all stoves when not in use. The Royal Society for the Prevention of Accidents publishes leaflets giving advice on this subject, and the HMSO pamphlet *Fire precautions in pleasure craft* (Home Office Fire Note 1/1966) gives detailed recommendations.

Fuel tanks and pipes. Expert advice and the best of materials and workmanship are needed if leakage under sea-going conditions is to be avoided. Good ventilation is needed in spaces containing fuel tanks and pipes to avoid the accumulation of vapour.

Electrical equipment. Electrical wires, batteries and charging motors need regular attention. A chafed wire can easily spark and create a fire hazard.

Ropes and rigging. Wires, ropes, fairleads and rigging generally need to be stronger and heavier for work in the open sea, possibly for days at a time, than would be required for shorter passages. In sailing craft, chafe is a great destroyer of gear and precautions must be taken to keep it to a minimum. It is important that the equipment used is designed for the job and that spares are carried.

Openings in the hull. Water intakes or soil pipes should be kept in perfect condition, and if below or near the water line, should be fitted with sea cocks. It should always be remembered that polythene thrown into the water can obstruct pipes or foul propellers.

Manning

The person in charge of a vessel cruising with young people should have considerable experience in the sort of voyage projected and in the type of craft to be used. At least a proportion of the crew should have made a number of short passages before an extended cruise is attempted. A suitably experienced assistant should be available if the size of the vessel or the duration of the voyage justifies it. At least one member of the crew should be able to prepare hot meals at sea. The total ship's company should not exceed ᵗhe number which can be carried comfortably having regard to the length of time to be spent at sea. Fatigue is the great enemy of safety. At least one member of the crew should be qualified in first aid and suitable equipment should be carried.

Members of staff who intended to sail off-shore should be encouraged to obtain the RYA/DOT Yachtmaster (Offshore) Certificate, details of which are in RYA publication G15.

Preparation
A cruise should be prepared meticulously. The following points are important:

a. During the months preceding a cruise, the person in charge and as many of the crew as possible should take every opportunity to increase their skills in navigation and seamanship. Many local authorities and other bodies run courses in these subjects.

b. During this period everything possible should be done to put the vessel to be used in the best possible condition. If the crew is involved in this work their knowledge of their ship will be improved.

c. Before sailing, a voyage plan with estimated times of arrival and departure should be communicated to coastguards (see Coastal etc. passages, paragraph e, page 29), harbour authorities and others who will keep a watch and act in the event of serious delay. This should be revised as necessary during the voyage and the various authorities informed. It is important that at each stage of the voyage an alternative plan should be arranged in advance to cover such eventualities as taking shelter in a convenient harbour or refuge. It is wise to have some one person, probably at the home port, who can maintain these contacts and follow the progress of the voyage. He should always be informed of departure and arrival times.

d. Food, water, fuel and stores should be stocked for considerably more than the expected time at sea.

e. Though plans may be made for daylight passages only, navigation lights, compass and chart should always be carried.

f. All gear and equipment should be carefully checked before sailing. As in small boat work, a 'checklist' is necessary.

g. Insurance policies should be checked to ensure that they cover the planned activity.

Safety measures
The following ideas will be found to be generally useful and indicate the need to maintain an active discipline:

a. Apart from personal buoyancy (see Lifejackets, page 18), the use of which will depend upon the vessel and the weather conditions, each member of the crew should be provided with a safety harness, to BS 4224/1975, to be worn at all times and to be attached when under way and on deck.

b. Rules governing movement about the vessel at night, or when under way, should be established at the outset and strictly adhered to; for example, no one should ever be on deck alone.

c. Rules for the prevention of fire are of great importance.

d. Equipment such as bilge-pumps, auxiliary power, anchors, drogues and signalling apparatus should be used regularly to give practice and to ensure efficiency when the need arises.

e. Emergency drills such as 'man overboard', 'fire' and 'abandon ship', should be practised frequently and under as realistic conditions as possible. The crew's confidence in the equipment and in each other is a prime factor in preventing accidents from developing into disasters. If the crew is a large one a list of emergency duties assigned to each person should be drawn up and posted prominently.

f. A well-organised and active routine should be developed. Boredom can lead to mischief and thence to accidents.

g. The advantages of two or more vessels cruising in company cannot be overstressed.

Health

Sea voyages in comparatively small craft are often accompanied by cramped conditions, damp, discomfort and fatigue; only the physically fit should take part and care should be taken not to overtax their strength by too long a period at sea. Whenever possible, each leg of the voyage should be completed within a single day and should begin and end with a quiet night in harbour. Voyages should be short to start with and should only be lengthened as experience is gained and bodies become used to the hardships. Oilskins or some equally suitable waterproof clothing will be necessary for work in heavy weather.

Sailing information

In addition to the general preparation for the cruise, all available sources should be studied for information about each leg of the voyage. It is good practice to prepare in advance a resumé of courses, distances, sea marks and turning points, since work may be difficult when under way, though plastic covers on charts and chinagraph pencil are of value. The following sources of information should not be neglected.

a. The Meteorological Office and BBC for weather forecasts.

b. *Admiralty sailing directions* for the area.

c. The latest *Light list.*

d. *Current notices to mariners.*

e. Charts to the largest possible scale which should be corrected up to date.

f. Tide tables and tidal charts. Vessels of 12 metres length or more are covered by the *Merchant Shipping (Carriage of Nautical Publications) Rules, 1975,* available from Marine Division, Department of Trade.

g. Local sources of knowledge, e.g. fishermen, pilots, harbour masters and yacht clubs, though caution should be used as there may be a lack of understanding of the limitations of the crew.

It is always good practice to establish and record errors inherent in navigating instruments and to test them periodically for accuracy. This particularly applies to steering and bearing compasses, logs, depth recorders, sextants, chronometers and radio aids.

Records

It is wise to maintain a fairly full account of a cruise in the form of a log book. If this is done during short passages an abstract of the 'sins of omission and commission' can be made which will be of great value when preparing a more ambitious project.

Underwater swimming

Underwater swimming makes use of the water as an environment rather than as a surface on which to be active, and offers opportunities for educational activity as well as recreation which are proving to be of increasing interest to schools. As with sailing and canoeing there are basic safety requirements to be followed, and a wide variety of equipment available from which to choose. Advice and help is available through the governing body of the sport, the British Sub-Aqua Club, whose regional coaches arrange courses for teachers to obtain the snorkel instructor's certificate. Teachers holding this certificate may instruct and examine pupils to the level of the snorkeller award for children.

School and college clubs may apply to become branches of the BSAC Schools and Youth Federation, through which those of 15 years and over can progress to aqualung diving.

Addresses of bodies from which advice and information may be sought:

National School Sailing Association, Foxglove House, Shawfield Road, Wade Court, HAVANT, Hants.

British Schools Canoeing Association, Fairplay House, Wickham Bishops, WITHAM, Essex.

British Sub-Aqua Club, 70 Brompton Road, LONDON SW3 1HA.

British Canoe Union, 70 Brompton Road, LONDON SW3 1DT.

Royal Yachting Association, Victoria Way, WOKING, Surrey GU21 1EQ.

The Association of Sea Training Organisations, Victoria Way, WOKING, Surrey GU21 1EQ.

The Sports Council, 70 Brompton Road, LONDON SW3 1EX.

Royal Society for the Prevention of Accidents, Cannon House, The Priory, Queensway, BIRMINGHAM B4 6BS.

Royal Life Saving Society, 14 Devonshire Street, LONDON W1N 2AT.

Amateur Swimming Association, Fern House, LOUGHBOROUGH, Leics.

Department of Trade, Marine Division, Branch 2, Savoy Hill House, Savoy Hill, LONDON WC2R 0BX.

Safety Afloat: Check List

For LEA officers, advisers and heads of schools

1   Are you satisfied that those in charge of activities afloat are adequately qualified and experienced?

2   Do you issue standing orders which regulate water activities undertaken by schools to take account of local conditions and the best local knowledge available?

3   Are lifejackets always worn, and do they conform to BSI Specification No. 3595/1969?

4   Are escort boats adequately powered and equipped for the waters and conditions in which they may have to operate?

5   Are your schools members of the local or national School Sailing/Canoeing Association?

6   Is insurance cover adequate for all people and property involved, and is the person in charge of activities aware of any relevant conditions in the policy?

7   Do schools engaged in activities afloat also foster an interest among pupils in the awards of the Amateur Swimming Association and the Royal Life Saving Society?

8   Do those directly responsible for activities afloat inform you of any relevant recommendations in this chapter which they are unable to follow?

For persons directly responsible for school activities afloat

1   Do you know the temperature of the water in which your pupils may find themselves?

2   Does the water temperature influence the instructions you give about the disposition of craft and escort boat, and about the clothing to be worn?

3   Do you have good evidence that the pupils can swim competently in realistic conditions?

4   Can all your pupils carry out expired-air resuscitation?

5   Do pupils and staff alike wear BSI 3595/1969 lifejackets whenever they are afloat?

6   Do you inspect the conditions of lifejackets and ensure that they are correctly worn before pupils go afloat?

7   Do you frequently test the air-tightness of partially inflatable lifejackets?

8   Do you make sure that capsize drill has been thoroughly mastered before allowing pupils to go out without an instructor?

9   Is there a waterproofed check-list for each craft? Does a pupil in charge of a craft have to report that the check has been completed satisfactorily before departing?

10   Is the control of activities managed efficiently? Are there accessible records of which pupils are in each craft, their programme of activities, any limits imposed, and when they are due to return?

11   Are weather forecasts, sailing/canoeing limits, and tidal information required reading before setting out, and are pupils required to report their safe return?

12   Do you have a visual recall signal which can be clearly distinguished by craft at any position in the activity area, whatever the wind conditions?

13   Are all pupils and instructors aware of procedures for calling for help in the event of accidents?

14   Do the arrangements and procedures described in this chapter meet the particular circumstances of your own case?

These questions do *not* cover the additional requirements for extended inland passages, coastal work, or cruises.

3
Safety in the Air

Air education

For some years now school parties taking holidays abroad have travelled on scheduled and chartered flights and the use of this form of transport will increase. The advice given in this chapter is not related to safety precautions which are to be taken for this type of flying. This is more appropriately the concern of the national regulatory authorities, the airline company, the local education authority, the school, and parents. The information which follows is relevant to those occasions on which an aircraft is used, in effect, as an extension of the school classroom or as an alternative to sport and games played in or out of school time.

An increasing number of pupils of all ages view from the air the terrain they are covering in field studies, and aspects of the landscape related to their classroom work in history and geography. Many teachers also use the air medium to motivate children to learn and to provide illustrative material for the teaching of traditional subjects in the school curriculum. Where schools offer a CSE or GCE course in aeronautics this can involve pupils in flying in small aircraft and visiting airfields to reinforce their technical studies.

A number of local authorities arrange residential courses at gliding clubs and organise Junior Wings Schemes through which pupils are taught to fly powered aircraft. The construction of hovercraft has also been undertaken by schools and many of the safety regulations related to aircraft apply to these vehicles.

In all these activities some element of risk must be acccepted but the adoption of certain reasonable safety precautions and an understanding of the basic principles of the operation of aircraft will minimise the risk of accidents.

The relevance of this form of education to the air and space age is instanced by the formation of the Air Education and Recreation Organisation (AERO) to advise and encourage authorities and teachers on all aspects of its use.

General precautionary measures

The importance of detailed and careful planning well before the intended flight or visit cannot be over-emphasised. The following precautions should be taken before engaging in any airborne activities:

Insurance: Flying, gliding and parachuting clubs are generally covered for third-party risk only, and personal insurance, if required, should be arranged by the participant, his parent, or the party collectively. The local education authority's own insurance cover for school parties on educational visits or school journeys may possibly give individual cover for flying and gliding, but the organiser of the party or the person in charge should have consulted the local education authority and know precisely what insurance cover there is from this source.

Consent: Where applicable the written consent of the parent or guardian of the participant should be obtained before he engages in the sport.

Powered flight

General safety precautions

The following precautions should be taken when organising flights by parties of school pupils:

All operators of aircraft of over 5,000 lb maximum weight used for the purpose of public transport (that is in general, where fares are charged) must hold an air operator's certificate. If an aircraft carries seven or more passengers it will usually be over 5,000 lb maximum weight, and must be operated under the terms of the air operator's certificate. Anyone proposing to take parties of young people on an educational flight should therefore make certain that the operator of the aircraft holds this certificate.

When a small aircraft (that is, one of maximum weight of 5,000 lb or less) is used, the school organiser of the flight should check that the aircraft is certified and maintained and operated to public transport requirements.

The organiser, or a teacher fully briefed by the organiser, should fly with the group.

The organiser of the party should give to the operator of the aircraft the fullest information about the purpose of the flight so that the pilot can be briefed on the educational nature of the exercise and of the requirements of the party.

The captain of the aircraft, with this background information, will then be able to brief the party on what to expect during the flight, on what flying conditions are likely and on some of the limitations of the aircraft when used for this special educational purpose. At the same time he will be able to issue instructions on matters such as movement about the aircraft, access to the flight deck and general conduct and discipline during the flight.

Where such a briefing by the captain, member of the crew or cabin staff is not possible, the organiser should obtain the necessary information and himself give the briefing. He will, in any case, have touched on several of these matters at the time of classroom preparation but must impress on everyone the requirement of discipline in obeying any instructions given by the flying crew or staff.

NB Should arrangements be made for pupils to fly with a person holding a private pilot's licence or a professional pilot's licence not endorsed for the appropriate aircraft *no form of payment must be made.* In such a case particular consideration should be given to the experience of the pilot and special conditions of insurance cover.

Ground safety measures

   a. At all times the organiser of the party will make himself familiar with local safety regulations and see that they are carried out.
   b. The strictest discipline is demanded of the party when walking between the terminal building and aircraft.
   c. Generally, and certainly with large parties, this movement should be under the direct supervision of a member of the staff of the aircraft operator.
   d. All clothing, exercise books, maps, papers, etc., must be firmly secured in case engine slipstream is encountered. The retrieving of any object blown away must be done with the utmost care by a member of staff as there is a great deal of ground traffic at a busy airport.

Construction of powered flying machines

Any educational establishment proposing to build a powered flying machine should consult the Civil Aviation Authority before starting construction, for advice on the requirements to be met. These are stringent, and a school proposing such a project should be thoroughly aware of the facilities required and the time involved in constructing an aircraft. It must never be flown until either a permit to fly or a certificate of airworthiness has been issued, and then only by a suitably licensed and approved pilot.

Hovercraft

Though there are at present no mandatory regulations covering the construction of home-built hovercraft for private use, careful consideration must be given to safety precautions both in their manufacture and operation. Before starting a hovercraft project the *Safety requirements for construction and operation of hovercraft* issued by the Hoverclub of Great Britain should be studied.

Gliding

There is an increasing participation in gliding as a form of physical recreation. In his first approach to a club the organiser of gliding (whether under the auspices of a school or not) should find out whether the club is affiliated to the British Gliding Association, the national administration body. Affiliation means that the club meets the Association's requirements.

The organiser should also satisfy himself that:

the gliders to be used have certificates of airworthiness and are maintained to BGA standards;

the person instructing in the air has an instructor's category;

the launching equipment is of a satisfactory standard;

the club field has a good hazard-free landing area: this is essential if it is intended that pupils fly solo.

Although no special dress is necessary the gliding pupil must be properly equipped for the weather. In winter it can be extremely cold on the field, and warm windproof clothing and appropriate footwear are essential. In hot summer weather a head covering is advisable.

The person in charge must be sensitive to natural feelings of nervous tension in the early stages of learning to fly and no pupil should be forced to fly against his wishes.

Safety on the ground

Participants must be thoroughly conversant with the rules of the club for the operation of gliders.

Some of the main precautions are:

a. At all times pupils must do exactly what the instructor orders. This applies to instruction by the winch driver, cable retriever, and any person in charge of a ground activity concerned with gliding.
b. The landing approach of a glider is soundless. At all times on the field a pupil must keep a look-out for approaching gliders.
c. Ground discipline and good team-work mean more flying and therefore there is all the more reason to pay attention to safety precautions.

d.   Pupils must not stand or walk in front of a glider about to be launched or coming in to land.

e.   Pupils must learn to park a glider correctly and must not move it without permission from the flying instructor or the owner of the aircraft.

f.   A glider on the ground can easily be damaged if it is held or pushed at an incorrect pace. Should a pupil see any damage or feel that some damage may have been done it must be reported at once so that an appropriate inspection can be made.

g.   The launching cable must not be handled except under express order by the instructor and a finger should never be put through the ring at the end of the cable.

h.   Where there is aero-towing of gliders, pupils must not pass in front of a powered aircraft when the engine is running and must keep well clear of the propeller even when it is stopped. They should know also that pilot visibility from a single engine aircraft which is stationary or taxiing is often restricted.

Safety in the air

The flying instructor is in charge of glider and pupil. He is responsible for the teaching of safety precautions but the following general points should be observed prior to take-off.

a.   When getting into or out of the glider care must be taken to step only on those parts of the aircraft reinforced specifically for this purpose.

b.   Safety harness must be correctly worn and must never be undone during flight.

c.   Small pilots will need cushions.

d.   The correct method of attachment of the cable to the glider must be learned by all pupils.

e.   The correct method of signalling for glider take-off must be known.

Construction of gliders by educational establishments

Schools attracted towards gliding and interested in glider construction should obtain technical information and advice from the British Gliding Association before embarking on a project. In addition to the high financial outlay the construction of a glider calls for many months of highly skilled effort, appropriate tools, an adequately heated workshop and considerable technical knowledge on the part of the person in charge. Continuous inspection by an inspector approved by the British Gliding Association or the Civil Aviation Authority is obligatory.

Parachuting
Some establishments may wish to consider sport parachuting as a recreation. For parachute jumping the minimum age is 17 years. To ensure the maximum degree of safety in these sports a rigid code of discipline and adherence to regulations, in addition to a high level of physical fitness, are required.

Before introducing this sport contact should be made with the British Parachute Association for information on the regulations and the relevant rules for the formation of a club or group.

Hang gliding
Since its introduction in recent years there has been a rapid increase in the number of people taking part in this adventurous sport. Much of the attraction has been the opportunity to fly at a relatively low cost through the individual effort of the participant making use of geographical features and atmospheric conditions. The British Hang Gliding Association has been formed to control the development of the sport and determine safety requirements and standards.

There is an element of risk in hang gliding as there is in all adventurous sports. This risk can be minimised by rigid adherence to the code of behaviour produced by the national body. The need for a strict code of discipline cannot be over-emphasised and development of the regulations controlling the sport cannot be achieved without the co-operation of all.

Hang gliding is a strenuous activity and participants need to be extremely active and physically fit. The minimum age for solo flying is 16 years and where applicable the consent of parents should be obtained before anyone takes part in the sport.

Before introducing hang gliding, organisers should contact the British Hang Gliding Association for general information, advice on sites, the approval and suitability of gliders and the safety considerations relating to operations.

Insurance
Organisers must check the insurance position with the LEA before allowing anyone to become involved.

Parascending
There is a developing interest in this sport. CCF units and scout groups at

some schools have formed clubs, and interest may spread to other groups in schools, colleges and youth organisations.

The participant uses a parachute canopy similar in appearance to that used in free fall parachuting, but starts with the parachute deployed and uses a tow line from a moving vehicle to gain height. In this way a trainee can be gently introduced to the sensation of parachuting while under the control of the instructor in the towing vehicle, gradually gaining experience until capable of releasing the tow line and completing a free fall.

The sport is controlled by a national body, the British Association of Parascending Clubs, who determine the regulations controlling the sport and license instructors. Any educational establishment interested in the sport should contact the BAPC to obtain the regulations and addresses of sites of recognised clubs.

To minimise the risk in a sport of this nature it is essential that the regulations and codes of discipline laid down by the national body are rigidly adhered to and that only instructors licensed by that body are employed in training students.

There is at present no age limit for participation but organisers should consider carefully the physical requirements of the sport before agreeing to its introduction.

Where applicable the consent of parents must be obtained before anyone takes part.

Insurance

Though the risk of injury is not high in well-conducted clubs there is not yet sufficient evidence to permit fair judgement. Organisers must check the insurance position with the LEA before allowing anyone to take part.

Addresses:

Air Education and Recreation Organisation, Carwarden House, 118 Upper Chobham Road, CAMBERLEY, Surrey.

British Association of Parascending Clubs, B/M Parascending, LONDON WC1V 6XX.

The British Gliding Association, Kimberley House, 47 Vaughan Way, LEICESTER LE1 4SG.

British Hang Gliding Association, Monksilver, TAUNTON, Somerset.

The British Parachute Association Limited, Kimberley House, 47 Vaughan Way, LEICESTER LE1 4SG.

The Civil Aviation Authority (Airworthiness Division), Brabazon House, REDHILL, Surrey.

Hoverclub of Great Britain Limited, 12 Lind Street, RYDE, IoW.

Safety in the Air: Check List

All educational and recreational flights, parachuting and parascending

1   Have parents been informed of the kind of activities in which participants will be involved and where necessary given their permission?
2   Has the insurance position been checked with the LEA?
3   Do all participants understand the need for rigid adherence to the rules and regulations governing the activity?

Powered flying

1   Does the aircraft operator comply with the licensing regulations?
2   Have the educational purposes of the flight been discussed with the aircraft operator and any special conditions agreed?
3   Have local ground and air safety procedures been obtained?
4   Have other staff members taking part been briefed on the purpose and conduct of the flight?
5   Have the participants been briefed on the behaviour and safety precautions required on the ground and in the air?

Gliding

1   Are the participants wearing suitable clothing?
2   Has the operation of gliding been explained?
3   Do they understand the dangers of cables and winches?
4   Where powered aircraft are used are participants aware of the procedure and possible dangers?
5   Has the team work for the safe handling of gliders on the ground been taught?

Hang gliding

1   Are the site, hang glider and instructor approved by the BHGA?
2   Are the participants wearing the correct clothing?
3   Are the participants thoroughly conversant with the rules laid down by BHGA?

Parachuting

1   Are the participants wearing correct clothing?

2   Are the instructor and equipment approved by the BPA?

Parascending
1   Are the site, equipment and instructor approved by BPAC?
2   Are the participants wearing the correct clothing?
3   Are the participants thoroughly conversant with the rules laid down by BAPC?
4   Has the policy on age of participants been adhered to?

Construction of aircraft and hovercraft
1   Have the regulating authorities been consulted?
2   Are the constructional regulations understood?
3   Have the licensing requirements of pilot or driver been complied with?

Appendix A: National Parks

Area	Youth and Schools Liaison Officer or other contact
Brecon Beacons	The Information Officer Brecon Beacons National Park Glamorgan Street BRECON Powys LD3 7DR Telephone: Brecon 2673 Ext 6 (STD 0874)
Dartmoor	The National Park Officer Dartmoor National Park Devon County Council County Hall Topsham Road EXETER EX2 4OD Telephone: Exeter 77977 (STD 0392)
Exmoor	Youth and Schools Liaison Office Exmoor National Park Department Exmoor House DULVERTON Somerset Telephone: Dulverton 665
Lake District	Youth and Schools Liaison Officer Lake District National Park Brockhole National Park Centre Nr WINDERMERE Westmorland Telephone: Windermere 2231 Ansafone service on local weather conditions in the Lake District Up to the end of March: weekends only From the end of March operates every day Telephone: Windermere 5151/2
Northumberland	The Information Officer Northumberland National Park Department Bede House All Saints Office Centre NEWCASTLE UPON TYNE NE1 1SA Telephone: Newcastle 610796 (STD 0632)

North York Moors

Information Officer
North York Moors National Park
The Old Vicarage
Bondgate
HELMSLEY
Yorkshire
Telephone: Northallerton 3123 (STD 0609)

Peak District

Youth Liaison Assistant
Peak Park Planning Board
Alcern House
Baslow Road
BAKEWELL
Derbyshire DE4 1AE
Telephone: Bakewell 2881 (STD 062 981)

Pembrokeshire Coast

Assistant Information Officer (Field)
Pembrokeshire Coast National Park
County Planning Department
County Offices
HAVERFORDWEST
Telephone: Haverfordwest 3131 (STD 0437)

Snowdonia

Youth and Schools Liaison Officer
Snowdonia Park
Information Service
Yr Hen Ysgol
Maentwrog
BLAENAU FFESTINIOG
Merionethshire
Telephone: Maentwrog 274 (STD 076 685)

Yorkshire Dales

Information Officer
Yorkshire Dales National Park
Colvend
GRASSINGTON
Yorks
Telephone: Grassington 748 (STD 075 674)

Printed in England for Her Majesty's Stationery Office
by The Campfield Press, St. Albans

Dd 586751 K80 4/77